Statistical Tricks and Traps

An Illustrated Guide to the Misuses of Statistics

Ennis C. Almer

Illustrations by
Louie Joseph Cantal

Pyrczak Publishing

P.O. Box 39731 • Los Angeles, CA 90039

Although the author and publisher have made every effort to ensure the accuracy and completeness of information contained in this book, we assume no responsibility for errors, inaccuracies, omissions, or any inconsistency herein. Any slights of people, places, or organizations are unintentional.

Editorial assistance provided by Brenda Koplin, Sharon Young, Cheryl Alcorn, Elaine Fuess, and Randall R. Bruce.

Special thanks to Ron Matossian, California State University, Los Angeles, who provided many helpful comments on the first draft of this book.

Cover design by Robert Kibler and Larry Nichols.

Printed in the United States of America.
10 9 8 7 6 5 4 3 2 1   DOC   07 06 05 04 03 02 01 00 99

ISBN 1-884585-23-X

Contents

Continued →

Introduction

As an applied branch of mathematics, statistical analysis is straightforward and non-controversial. For example, if a researcher calculates a percentage, his or her calculations can be double-checked by others, and assuming care was used in performing the calculations, all the checks will match the researcher's original answer. Yet, there are dangers in using statistics that derive from two sources:

- *Statistical Tricks*: These occur when researchers deliberately attempt to mislead their readers.

  Sometimes tricks are accomplished by drawing a misleading graph or through the inappropriate selection of statistics. For example, there are three different averages (as you will learn in this book). The inappropriate selection of one average over the others could be misleading.

  At other times, tricks are based on the use of inappropriate research methods used to generate the data for statistical analysis. For example, a peculiar sample of respondents might be deliberately chosen for a survey to produce a desired result.

- *Statistical Traps*: A researcher falls into a statistical trap when he or she naively or carelessly misapplies statistical methods or employs unsound research methods to generate statistical data. While a trap is not intentional, it can produce highly misleading results.

How to Avoid Tricks and Traps

After reading this book, you will be able to spot certain types of trick or traps such as misleading graphs.

Unfortunately, many of the tricks and traps cannot be directly spotted because only the end result—not the raw data—are usually reported. However, this book will teach you what types of important questions researchers should address in their reports, and you will learn to take their results with a large grain of salt if they are not addressed.

The Philosophy Underlying This Book

Three premises underlie the development of this book. First, statistical methods are useful. They help us make decisions in almost all fields of modern life from medicine to education. Second, many statistics are misleading (whether or not it is intentional). Third, all people can be taught how to protect themselves from misleading statistics by learning the rudiments of statistics and research methods presented in this book.

Suggestions for Using This Book

The material in this book is highly non-technical and requires no prior training in statistics. Hence, the book is an ideal supplement for use in survey courses such as introductory psychology, sociology, or business. It is also ideal as a jump-start for courses in statistics since the book gives an overview of the major issues confronting statisticians, which can be mastered during the first week or two of a semester.

When used as a supplementary book, instructors may wish to assign students to bring in examples of statistical reporting that is misleading (such as a misdrawn graph) or suspicious because of the failure to address the major issues raised in this book (for example, failure to indicate how a sample was drawn). Both types of examples can be found in both the popular media and in research reports published in academic journals. Such an assignment might be a required part of the course or used for extra credit.

The Big Picture

Tricks or Traps 26 and 27 illustrate why it is important to get the big picture by examining the *body* of research on a topic. While any one research report may easily be based on faulty statistical methods, a body of research conducted independently by various researchers (each of whom is subject to different traps) is much more likely to be reliable. Because this principle is so important, it would be appropriate to read Tricks or Traps 26 and 27 first and then *reread* them again at the end.

Communicating with Me

Your reactions to this book would be greatly appreciated. Criticisms and additional examples that might be used to improve the Second Edition are especially welcome.

I hope you enjoy this book and become a better consumer of statistical reporting along the way.

Ennis C. Almer

If you can't convince them, confuse them!

–Harry S. Truman

Trick or Trap 1

Which On-line Bookstore Is Largest?

There is an ongoing debate over which on-line bookstore is the largest. Of course, there are many ways in which "largeness" can be defined. Should it be the number of titles in stock ready for immediate shipment? Or should it be the number of books on hand including duplicate copies of popular books? Maybe it should be the number of square feet devoted to the storage of books. Until we can agree on a standard for determining largeness, we won't be able to answer the seemingly simple question posed at the top of this page.

For the sake of this example, let's use this standard: The largest bookstore is the one with the largest number of titles in its database. Having books in a database (although not necessarily in stock in a warehouse) has some advantages for consumers. Having a title in a database means that the bookstore can quickly provide consumers with information on pricing, format (for example, paperback vs. hardback), and availability.

As it turns out, the number of books in the database is exactly what one of the major on-line bookstores suggested as the standard for judging which bookstore is largest. (We'll call this bookstore *BIB* for the *Bigger-Is-Better Bookstore*.) In fact, *BIB* took out a full-page advertisement in a popular magazine to make the claim that it had about twice as many books in its database than its main competitor, which we'll call *HIP* for the *Huge-Impresses-People Bookstore*. So far, so good, but here's the trick or trap: In its advertisement, *BIB* included a graph similar to the one shown in Figure 1. Notice that the bar for *BIB* is not only twice as tall, it is also twice as wide as the one for *HIP*, creating the *visual* impression that *BIB* is much more than twice as large as *HIP*. Figure 2 illustrates how it should have been drawn, with bars of equal width.

The lesson: Increasing *both* the height and width causes a geometric increase in overall area. Read the fine print. Don't rely solely on the visual impression created by a bar graph.

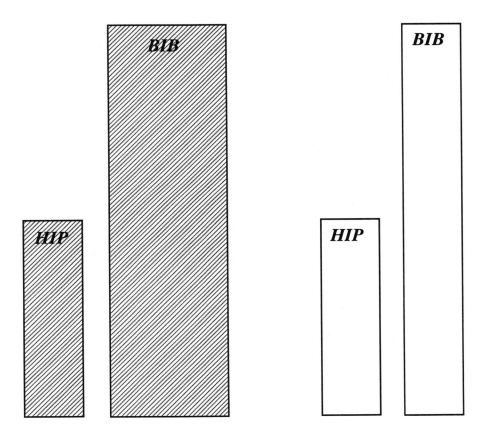

Figure 1
Misleading:
Twice as tall and twice as wide.

Figure 2
Correct:
Twice as tall only creates
a figure with twice the area.

Trick or Trap 2

Most Pickups Still on the Road?

A major automobile manufacturer ran a full-page advertisement claiming that five years after being manufactured, a larger percentage of its pickups were still on the road—when compared with its two major competitors. This certainly should be of interest to consumers. However, while the differences were quite small, the advertisement contained a graph that magnified them. The graph was similar to the one shown in Figure 1 in which the differences look pretty impressive until you consider that the bars start at a base of 90% and go up to only 93%, as indicated in Figure 2.

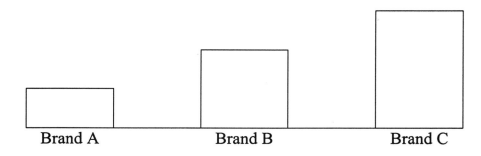

Figure 1 *Misleading:*
Small percentage differences illustrated with large differences among the bars.

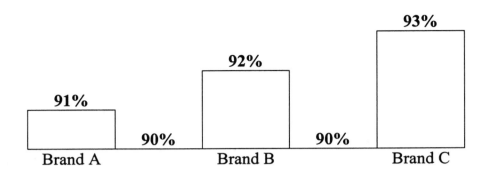

Figure 2 *Percentages for Figure 1 shown in bold. Still misleading:*
Small percentage differences illustrated with large differences among the bars.

To avoid such misleading drawings, they should begin at a base of zero, as shown in Figure 3.

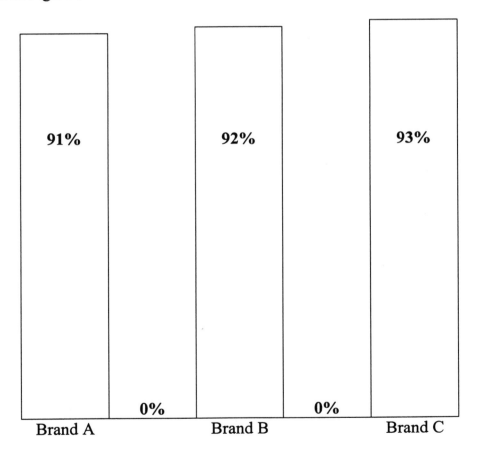

Figure 3 *Correct:*
Small percentage differences illustrated with *small* differences among the bars. Base starts at zero percent.

Trick or Trap 3

100% of the Women in the Workforce?

Statisticians often use past trends to predict future ones. Often, this is done with a line graph that shows the previous trends with a solid line and the projection with a dashed line. Figure 1 shows this for the data on the percentage of women in the workforce from 1970 to 1980 when the percentage increased from about 47% to about 58%. Making a "straight-line projection," we reach the false conclusion that 100% of the women will be in the workforce around the year 2020.

What can we do to avoid misleading predictions of future behavior based on trend lines? First, we should recognize that such projections are based on the fundamental assumption that the dynamics underlying the past behavior will remain the same in the future. Examples of underlying dynamics for women joining the workforce include economic forces (such as employment growth) and societal attitudes toward women working.

Second, we can look at longer-term trends. In our example, we can look at growth in previous decades. For example, from 1940 to 1950, there was very little growth in the percentage of women in the workforce. Knowing that in some decades there is more growth and in others there is less, tempers any projections we are tempted to make.

Third, we should modify long-term projections by applying common sense. For example, it is common sense that there is a certain percentage of women who will never join the workforce for a variety of reasons such as being physically or mentally ill, being incarcerated, or simply not needing or wanting to work. Thus, in our example, it makes sense that the percentage of women in the workforce will hit an upper ceiling substantially below 100%.

Fourth, we can keep in mind that an upward trend is more sustainable when there is more room for growth. For example, with only about 47% of the women in the workforce in 1970, there were many women not yet in the workforce who might join it. As the percentage increases, there are fewer nonworking women to fuel the growth.

Fifth, we can ask whether there are any other statistics that might be used to justify growth projections. For example, surveys of female high school students' future occupational plans might provide information that would assist in making more accurate projections.

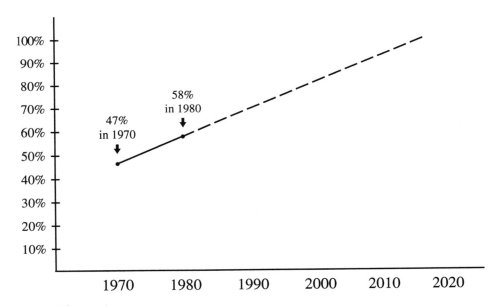

Figure 1
Misleading: Straight-line projection to 100%.
Note: Women aged 20 to 64 years in the workforce.

Trick or Trap 4

Who Wants Bottled Water?

A major metropolitan newspaper ran an article with a bar graph labeled "Thirst for Bottled Water." It showed California as tops with 788.2 million gallons of bottled water sold in a recent year. Eight other states were shown, but to keep our example straightforward, let's consider only one other: Arizona, as shown in Figure 1.

Let's suppose we want to open a bottled-water store to sell premium brands of bottled water as well as accoutrements such as designer bottled-water holders. In which state would we have a better chance of success? Well, at first glance, it might appear that California wins hands down until we consider that California has a population of about 30 million based on the latest census, and Arizona has a population of 3.7 million.

Dividing 788.2 (million gallons) by 30 (million people) for California, we obtain a rate of 26.3 gallons per person. For Arizona, the arithmetic yields 26.6 gallons per person. In other words, *per capita* (per person) consumption is about the same in the two states, as illustrated by Figure 2. So other things being equal (such as locating our store in an equally busy shopping mall in either state), we should expect the populations of the two states to be about equally receptive to the merchandise offered in our store.

What's the lesson here? When comparing two groups of unequal size, we should use a *rate* such as per capita consumption. Another popular rate is percentage, a statistic that we will consider in the next section of this book.

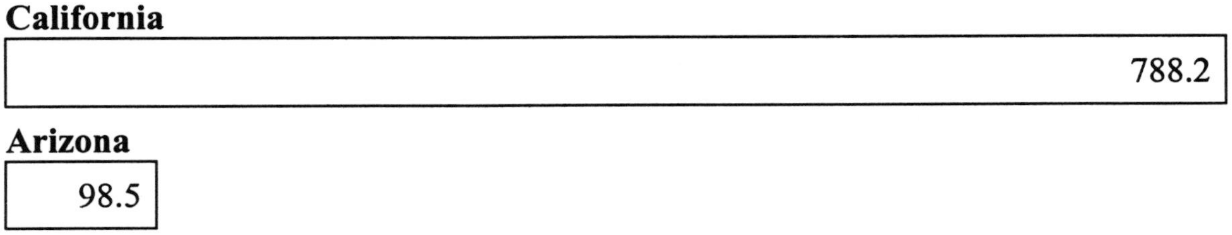

California

788.2

Arizona

98.5

Figure 1 *Potentially misleading*
Gallons of bottled water consumed (in millions)

California

26.3

Arizona

26.6

Figure 2 *Correct*
Gallons of bottled water consumed *per capita* (per person)

Trick or Trap 5

A Flat Tax or an Unfair Tax?

A newspaper ran a story on a city's efforts to collect business taxes from home-based businesses, which tend to be quite small. Among other things, the newspaper reporter stated, "The rates vary according to which of 40 business categories a company falls under. In all categories, however, the rate comes to less than 1% of gross receipts."

This tax is applied to *gross receipts*, that is, money collected by a business before expenses. Notice that it is *not* applied to *profits*, which are gross receipts less expenses. In addition, there is a minimum tax of $118.25.

Let's consider Tax Category A, for which the tax rate is .0018% of gross receipts. Jenny Smart, who established a home-based software company several years ago, now has gross receipts of $100,000 for the year. Her tax is $180.00 (that is, $100,000 x .0018 = $180). What the newspaper said is true for Jenny: She paid less than 1%.

Now let's consider Bobby Sloth whose first-year software business has yielded gross receipts of only $7,000. Let's calculate his taxes: $7,000 x .0018 = $12.60. But he does *not* owe $12.60; instead, he must pay the minimum of $118.25, which is 1.69% of his gross receipts. (Notice that $118.25 divided by $7,000 yields 1.69%). So Bobby's taxes are considerably *more than* the "less than 1%" cited by the newspaper.

Table 1 shows what we've considered so far.

Table 1 *Comparison of taxes paid on gross receipts*

	Gross receipts	Tax rate	Tax based on tax rate of .0018	Actual taxes paid (Note: *Minimum* of $118.25)	Percentage of gross receipts paid in taxes
Jenny	$100,000	.0018	$180.00	$180.00	0.18%
Bobby	$7,000	.0018	$12.60	$118.25	1.69%

Now let's see what effect the flat tax with a minimum has on Bobby's *profits*:

> Because it was a start-up business, Bobby had many expenses and needed to advertise heavily. He had gross receipts of $7,000 and expenses of $6,900, for a *profit* of $100.00. Since Bobby has to pay the minimum tax of $118.25, his entire profit of $100.00 (plus another $18.25 out of his pocket) goes to the city in taxes—for a tax rate of more than 100% of his *profits*—leaving him with no after-tax profits.

What we've seen in this example is that the author of the newspaper article failed to recognize that a "flat" percentage rate is deceptive if there is a minimum charge. Note that this is not an isolated example. For instance, credit card companies often charge a small percentage (such as 2%) with a minimum (such as $10) when people take cash advances against their cards. Someone who takes a small cash advance, such as $100, will be charged $10, which is 10% of the amount advanced.[1]

---

[1] Note that a minimum may be justified since the lender incurs expenses in making the cash advance loan, which must be processed. Also note that in the example on taxes, the city charges a registration fee of $25 in addition to taxes. Therefore, the minimum tax is not a fee-for-service since this is covered by the registration fee.

Trick or Trap 6

Shocking Increase in Cocaine Use?

According to the federal government's recent National Household Survey on Drug Abuse, the percentage change in use of cocaine by 12- to 17-year-olds was a shocking +167%, as reported in a national weekly news magazine.

A closer look at the underlying percentages reveals a somewhat more tempered story. At the beginning of the three-year period, 0.3% (three-tenths of one percent) reported trying cocaine. At the end of the three-year period, 0.8% reported trying it. Notice that in both years, the percentage remained less than 1%.

If you are having a hard time understanding where the 167% increase comes from mathematically, consider this: If it went from 0.3% to 0.6%, that would be a 100% increase (it would be double). In fact, it went from 0.3% to 0.8% (almost tripled for a 167% increase).

Of course, any increase in cocaine use by adolescents is cause for concern. However, we should keep in mind that this particular increase is quite small and might be accounted for in large measure by inaccuracies in polling. All polls are presumed to be off by at least a small amount because of errors such as the selection of only a random sample of households to contact, the current state of mind of the respondents, failure of some respondents to answer some questions, and so on. If the first poll in our example was off a small amount and *underestimated* cocaine use while the second poll three years later was off a small amount and *overestimated* its use, much of the observed increase could be attributed to the errors inherent in conducting polls. Clearly, longer-term data would be desirable before jumping to important conclusions regarding this issue.

The government reported about a +10% percentage increase in adolescents trying cigarettes over the same three-year period. The beginning percentage was 18.4% and the ending one was 20.2%. (In other words, 20.2 is about 10% higher than 18.4.)

Table 1 shows the statistics that we've considered so far.

Table 1 *Government statistics on substance use*

Substance	Percentage trying the substance in year one	Percentage trying the substance in year three	Difference from year one to year three	*Percentage increase*
Cocaine	0.3%	0.8%	0.5%	167%
Tobacco	18.4%	20.2%	1.8%	10%

Let's look at the data another way. To keep it simple, let's assume that there are only 1,000,000 12- to 17-year-olds in the country. Some basic arithmetic shows us *how many* reported trying each substance in each year (for example, .184 x 1,000,000 = 184,000 for reporting tobacco in year one). This type of arithmetic yields the *numbers* of adolescents, which are shown in Table 2. From the last column, it is clear that in terms of sheer *numbers*, the increase in tobacco use was much more substantial than the increase in cocaine use.

Table 2 *Numbers of adolescents using substances*

Substance	*Number* trying the substance in year one	*Number* trying the substance in year three	Difference from year one to year three
Cocaine	3,000	8,000	5,000
Tobacco	184,000	202,000	18,000

The lesson to be learned here is that when percentage increases are reported, always ask for the beginning and ending percentages. Also, consider the actual number of cases underlying the percentage increases.

Trick or Trap 7

What Is the Average Household Income?

As all students of statistics should know, there are several "averages." The two most common ones are the *mean* and the *median.* Because the misuse of averages can cause serious misinterpretations of data, it's important to understand their meanings and interpretations.

The mean is the most commonly used average. In fact, its use is so common that it is often simply called *the average.* To get the mean score of some students on a test, we add the scores and divide by the number of scores, as shown here:

Five scores: 5, 4, 3, 1, 7

Computation of the mean:
$5 + 4 + 3 + 1 + 7 = 20 \div 5 = 4.0$

As you can see, 4.0 is a good representation of the "typical" score *for this set of scores.*

Unfortunately, when there are some extreme scores, the mean can be pulled in their direction and take on a value that is not representative of the typical or center score. As an example, let's use the scores we just considered but assume that the student with a score of 7 now has a very high score of 95:

Five scores: 5, 4, 3, 1, 95

Computation of the mean:
$5 + 4 + 3 + 1 + 95 = 108 \div 5 = 21.6$

As you can see, 21.6 is not very representative since all the students except one had scores of 1 through 5. In other words, the one student with a score of 95 has undue influence on the value of the mean, which is supposed to represent the center of the group.

The median is the "middle score." To get it, we simply put the scores in order from low to high and count to the middle. Here are the scores that we just considered, put in order with an arrow showing the middle score.

Five scores, put in order from low to high: 1, 3, 4, 5, 95
↑
median

As you can see, the median is unaffected by the very high score of 95. In other words, it remains stable—providing an average that is typical of the majority of the students.

So let's now consider the question in the title of this topic: What is the average household income? It depends on which average you use. Here are the federal government's estimates for a recent year:

Mean household income: $48,165
Median household income: $35,536

As you can see, there's a very substantial difference between the two averages. So which one is more typical of U.S. households? The answer comes from knowledge of the distribution of incomes in the U.S. Specifically, there are very large numbers of households with low to moderate incomes (poor to middle class), but there are a relatively small number of households with very high incomes. These small numbers of rich and very rich have pulled up the *mean*. When talking about the typical income of the vast majority of the population, the *median* gives a more typical value. Put in more concrete terms, if we went about the country knocking on doors and asking people about their household income, we'd come across many more households with incomes of about $35,000 than households with incomes of about $48,000.

It should come as no surprise that the averages for variables related to income such as housing prices and the prices of automobiles can also be misrepresented by using the mean. In other words, the relatively small number of rich people tend to purchase very expensive houses and automobiles, which will pull up the mean for such items.

A lesson here: Don't settle for being told the "average." If possible, ask for both the mean and median. If the two have similar values, either may be used. If they have very different values, rely on the median.

Trick or Trap 8

In God They Trust?

In the previous topic, you learned about the *mean* and *median* and how they can give very different pictures of the average. In this topic, we'll consider a third average —the *mode*.

The mode has a simple definition: It is the most frequently occurring score. In other words, more people have this score than any other score. Let's consider an example. In a recent election cycle, analysis of the declaration speeches of those who were running for the presidency revealed the following number of references to God:

Number of references to God in declaration speeches of nine candidates: 1, 1, 1, 1, 2, 2, 2, 3, 14

The mode for this example is 1. That is, four candidates mentioned God one time, which is more than any other number of times. (Note that three candidates mentioned God two times, one mentioned God three times, and one mentioned God 14 times.)

What is the *mean* number of times? Here's the arithmetic:

Computation of the mean number of references to God:
$1 + 1 + 1 + 1 + 2 + 2 + 2 + 3 + 14 = 27 \div 9 = 3$

Next, let's consider the *median* value, as indicated here:

Nine scores in order from low to high. The score in the middle is the median:

1, 1, 1, 1, 2, 2, 2, 3, 14
            ↑
         median

So here are the three averages we've found for one set of data:

Type of average	
Mean	3
Median	2
Mode	1

Of the three values, the median (2) is arguably the most representative of the typical number of references to God. (The mode of 1 is at the bottom of the distribution, while the mean of 3 is near the top. An average should represent the "center.")

As you can see, there is clearly room for mischief here, given that there are three averages that have different values for the same set of data. A person could choose the average that most suited the point he or she was trying to make and simply call it "the average" number of references to God. As a general rule, be suspicious if someone reports what he or she calls the "average" since the person will be free to choose among the values and report the one that best supports his or her argument.

Note that the mean is very popular with academic researchers. Assuming they have checked to see that it is representative of a given set of scores, there is nothing wrong with using the mean. However, if someone you do not trust is reporting averages to you, it is best to ask for the *median* since it will provide a typical value even if the distribution of scores is skewed by some extreme values (such as the politician who mentioned God 14 times).

Trick or Trap 9

How Trusting Are Rape Survivors?

People citing research often make statements such as "Group A is higher (or lower) than Group B." Such statements are usually highly misleading since they make it sound as though all members of Group A are higher (or lower) than all members of Group B, which is usually not the case. A more accurate statement is *"On the average*, Group A is higher (or lower) than Group B."

Let's consider some real data that show an *average* difference for two groups.[1] One group consisted of 61 women who reported having been raped (rape survivors). These women were compared with a control group of 61 women. All the women were administered a personality test that measured their basic trust (trusting relationships, trusting others, etc.). The resulting data are shown in the table on the facing page, where higher scores indicate greater trust. Indeed, there is a difference: *On the average*, rape survivors (with a median of 40) exhibit less trust than the controls (with a median of 42). (You may recall that the *median* is one of the *averages* covered earlier in this book.)

Examining the actual data in the table, another fact jumps out at us: There is tremendous *variability* within both groups. In other words, there are large differences among the scores of the rape survivors; likewise, there are large differences among the controls. In addition, there is great *overlap* between the groups. Many of the rape survivors have basic trust scores that are higher than the controls. Thus, any discussion of the average difference should be moderated by a discussion of

---

[1] Data supplied by Stephen A. Karp, George Washington University.

variability and overlap between the groups. A simple way to do this would be to report the ranges for the two groups: Rape survivors have a range from 17 to 50 while the controls have a range from 20 to 50. In the next topic, we will consider another way to describe variability.

Score	Rape Survivors		Controls	
50	///// /		/////	
49				
48	////		///// //	
47	////		///	
46				
45	//		///// //	
44				
43	/////		///// ///	
42	///// /		////	←median
41			//	
40	///// //	←median	///// ///	
39				
38	/		/	
37	/		///// /	
36				
35	/////		//	
34				
33	//		/	
32	///// /			
31				
30	///		////	
29				
28	//		//	
27	//			
26				
25				
24				
23	//			
22				
21				
20	/		/	
19				
18				
17	//			

Trick or Trap 10

Draw a Happy Face?

Waiters and waitresses sometimes draw the ubiquitous happy face on the checks that they present to customers. In a study of whether this affects tips, a researcher had a waiter draw a happy face on the checks for about half his dining parties (24 parties) while not drawing it on those of the other half (21 parties).

The dining parties that had a happy face drawn on their checks had these percentage tips (that is, the percentage left by each dining party):[1]

Table 1 *Percentage tips when happy face was drawn on check (experimental group)*

31%	27%	26%	23%	23%	21%	21%	19%	18%	18%	17%	17%
17%	16%	15%	15%	15%	15%	14%	14%	13%	12%	9%	9%

For the data in Table 1, the *mean* tip was 18%. (You may recall from earlier in this book, the mean is a widely used average.)

For the group without happy faces, these are the percentage tips left by the dining parties:

Table 2 *Percentage tips when no happy face was drawn on check (control group)*

48%	40%	38%	33%	31%	27%	23%	23%	23%	22%	21%	21%
21%	20%	18%	16%	15%	9%	0%	0%	0%			

For the data in Table 2, the *mean* tip was 21%.

Thus, *on the average* when the waiter did *not* draw a happy face, he got higher tips (21%) than when he did draw a happy face (18%). However, it is clear from the data that the averages don't tell the whole story. In fact, reporting only the averages might be misleading because there is tremendous *variation* under

---

[1] Data supplied by Bruce Rind, Temple University.

each of the conditions, and this variation has led to great *overlap* in the percentages under the two conditions. Consider, for example, that even though Table 1 has a lower mean (18%), every percentage in that table is higher than the three lowest percentage tips in Table 2 (that is, the three parties that left 0%).

To avoid misinterpretation of means, they should be accompanied by standard deviations. The means and their standard deviations for the data we are considering are shown in Table 3.

Table 3 *Means and standard deviations for three conditions*

Condition	Mean	Standard Deviation (*sd*)
Happy face	18%	5
No happy face	21%	12

So what do the standard deviations tell us? First, that there was more variation in the no-happy-face condition (*sd* = 12) than in the happy-face-condition (*sd* = 5). We can confirm this by looking at the data in Tables 1 and 2. Notice that in Table 2 the percentages range from 0% to 48% (much variation), while in Table 1 they range only from 9% to 31% (less variation).

Second, the standard deviation gives us a rough guide to where the vast majority of the values lie.[2] For the happy-face condition with a mean of 18%, the standard deviation of 5 tells us that the vast majority of percentages are within about 5 points of 18% (that is, most are between 13% and 23%). For the no-happy-face condition, the vast majority lies within 12 points of 21% (that is, most are between 9% and 33%).

Table 4 shows what you've just learned:

Table 4 *Means, standard deviations, and interpretation of standard deviation*

Condition	Mean	Standard Deviation	Vast majority lies between
Happy face	18%	5	$18 \pm 5 =$ 13% and 23%
No happy face	21%	12	$21 \pm 12 =$ 9% and 33%

Looking at the last column of Table 4, you can see that there is great overlap between the two groups (that is, 13% to 23% overlaps with 9% to 33%). Keeping this in mind helps us avoid the oversimplification that would result if we considered only the mean percentages.

---

[2] If the distribution of scores forms a normal bell-shaped curve, the "vast majority" is defined as 68%.

Trick or Trap 11

How Many Internet Users?

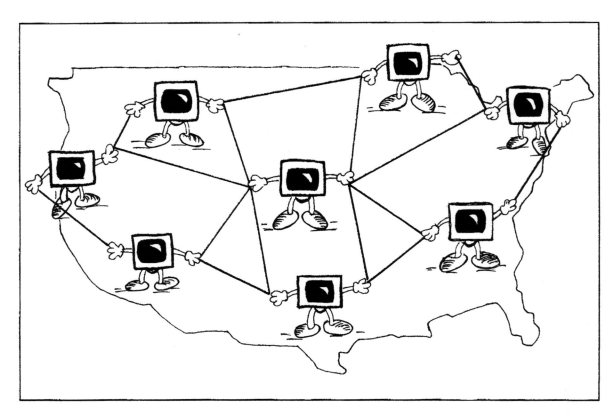

Back in the early days of widespread Internet usage (circa 1996), a major polling organization that we'll call Organization A conducted a national poll on Internet usage. It reported that there were about 24 million Internet users. At the time, this was a surprisingly large number and important news for people buying Internet stocks and for businesses interested in using the Internet for selling their goods and services.

A short time later, Organization B reported only about 9.5 million users—a number that is substantially different from the first one.

Both organizations used state-of-the art polling techniques, so why were the results so different? With hindsight, it appears to be a matter of definition. Here's the definition that Organization A used:

Any person who had used the Internet within the previous three months.

Here's the definition that Organization B used:

Any person currently using the Internet and who could name an Internet application besides e-mail.

In addition, Organization B found that only 35% of current users had visited 50 or more sites. Using 50 or more sites as a definition of people who are active Internet users (those who surf the Internet), the 9.5 million shrinks to 3.3 million (that is, 9.5 x .35 = 3.3).

Thus, the estimates range from 3.3 million to 24 million—depending on which definition is used!

The lesson is clear: When reading polls (and other reports of scientific investigations), knowing how key variables were defined is crucial. Other things being equal, put more faith in poll results when you are given the actual questions asked and the definitions that were used.

Trick or Trap 12

How Many Business Start-ups?

Let's suppose you rented a small store, obtained the appropriate city and state permits and licenses, purchased a quantity of flowers at wholesale prices, had a grand opening, and during your first year you grossed $50,000. You had no employees. Would you consider yourself to be in business? You might be surprised to learn that the U.S. Department of Labor would not define it as a business because you had no employees. Thus, your activities would not be classified as a new start-up for the year.

Using the *definition* that a business is a money-making activity *with employees*, the number of business start-ups in the country in a recent year was estimated to be about 800,000. However, when the Gallup Organization conducted a poll and allowed respondents to decide whether they had started a business (regardless of whether there were employees), the estimate was that there were about 3,500,000 business start-ups—that's more than four times as large as 800,000.

So which estimate is correct? It depends on the *definition*. The statistics are only as good as the definitions that underlie them. Let's consider two other definitions and some rough estimates of business start-ups for the same year. Poll respondents are allowed to self-define what a business is with the restrictions shown in italics below. In other words, if we take the 3,500,000 estimate and put some restrictions on it, we get these estimates:

> *A business is a money-making activity that takes place outside a home:*
> Roughly 381,150 start-ups.

> A business is a money-making activity *that has a business telephone line* (whether in a home or not):
> Roughly 1,200,000 start-ups.

We can't determine which of these definitions is best because it depends on the *purpose* for which the statistics are being collected. For example, for a poll conducted for a telephone company, the last definition might be of most interest. On the other hand, if the Internal Revenue Service (IRS) wanted an estimate of how many start-ups there were to compare the poll results with the number that were self-reported by taxpayers, a much broader definition might be in order, such as:

> Any activity other than making investments and being employed *that produces income.*

Producing income is crucial to our hypothetical definition for the IRS because that agency's function is to collect taxes on income.

The lesson, of course, is that the definitions underlying statistics are of utmost importance. Before putting too much faith in any particular result, be sure to inquire about the definition used and consider how it meshes with the purposes for which you will be using the results.

Trick or Trap 13

Whom Can You Trust?

When gathering data for statistical analysis, researchers make numerous assumptions. In fact, most are probably made at the subconscious level. Here's an example: Many years ago, Professor George Mahl had a research assistant administer some tests in a pilot study that would extend his work into a new area. The results were excitingly consistent with the professor's hypothesis. The statistics collected by the assistant would have been published except for the fact that when he asked two additional assistants to repeat the tests, the results did not agree with the original assistant's. Note that the professor was careful and conducted *replications* (repetitions of the study to see if the same results are obtained).

It is not uncommon in science for studies to fail to replicate. Things go wrong; a given study could be a fluke. In this particular case, the professor received a letter from the first research assistant fully 25 years later. This is part of the letter:

> I am writing to let you know that I consciously altered the results while measuring the response times to try and make the study support the hypothesis. I was very concerned at the time with the approval of others, and I felt that if the results supported your hypothesis, I would be more acceptable to you.
>
> I apologize for doing this and for jeopardizing your reputation....

As you can see, the professor made a reasonable assumption: That a research assistant would have no personal stake in the outcome of a scientific study and would honestly collect and report the data. Professor Mahl explains it this way:

> During some 40 years of active research, I had about 25 assistants. With each of them I took some form of care to ensure the accuracy of their work and that mistakes did not go undetected and uncorrected. At no time, however, did I imagine that any of them might deliberately falsify their work.[1]

Even seemingly minor and safe assumptions can dramatically alter the outcome of a study. Hence, it is important to have replications of studies—ideally conducted independently by other researchers.

---

[1] Excerpt from a letter to the editor of the *American Psychologist*, October 1995, pp. 882–883.

Trick or Trap 14

What's a Cool Face?

One of the major assumptions that underlies statistical studies is that the respondents understand the directions and questions they are given. Careful researchers try out their questions with small samples to test for understanding. Even with this precaution, major blunders sometimes occur.

Some years ago, I was in charge of coordinating the testing for a major project in which kindergarten and first-grade students' attitudes toward school needed to be measured. On each page of the students' test booklets there were three faces, as shown here:

Following the test maker's directions, children were told at the beginning of the testing session that the first face was the *happy face*, the second face was the *so-so face*, and the third face was the *sad face*. The test administrator would then read instructions such as "Put a mark on the face that shows how you feel when you come to school" and "Put a mark on the face that shows how you feel when you do your homework." Note that the faces were *not* explained again as these statements were read.

In my capacity as coordinator, I observed as many of the testing sessions as possible to check to see that the tests were being properly administered. I noticed that a number of children had puzzled looks on their faces as they worked through the test. After a number of testing sessions, I asked a sample of children individually to describe the meanings of the faces. *Not one child* identified the middle face as the "so-so face." Almost all just shrugged, some seemed embarrassed, and many said, "I don't know." However, one little boy said with great confidence, "That's the *cool* face." Now, as everyone in my generation knows, it's hip to be cool but it's not hip to be so-so.

What went wrong here? The test maker made the assumption that "so-so" was a concept that would be understood by such young children and would be meaningfully associated with the middle face. In quizzing about 30 children, I found none who could do this.

Trick or Trap 15

Unhealthy Water?

One summer, physicians in an East Coast town had an unusually large number of patients reporting nasty rashes. As with most new outbreaks of health problems, public health officials launched an investigation.

Specifically, they conducted an *after-the-fact* investigation to try to determine the cause of the rashes. After all, people already had the rashes (the fact), so the researchers attempted to do two things:

(1) determine what the people with the rashes had in common, such as things they ate and activities they participated in, and

(2) determine what things the people with rashes had in common that were *not* in common with other people without rashes.

Here's an example of how the statistical reasoning works: Suppose we found that all the people with rashes had eaten hot dogs (something they all had in common). This might point the finger at hot dogs. But also suppose that other patients who did *not* have rashes had also eaten the same brands of hot dogs. This would suggest that hot dogs did not cause the problem because both those with the rashes and those without rashes had eaten them. This type of research is known in scientific circles as *ex post facto* research (meaning, of course, *after-the-fact*).

Now, let's return to our real example involving the rashes. After numerous interviews, the investigators determined that the people with the rashes had all been swimming at a local lake (something in common). In addition, those patients who did *not* have rashes had *not* gone swimming there. So it seems like an open-and-shut case, right? The evidence clearly points to the water as the source of the problem, so signs were posted, and the word was spread to avoid the water.

Still, a number of new people were getting rashes even though they had not gone swimming in the lake. These new people were interviewed, and the investigators found that what they had in common was *visiting* the lake in order to sunbathe, picnic, and do all the things people do near lakes in the summer *except* swim. A physical investigation at the lake revealed that there was an organism in the soil around the lake that was causing the skin irritation. The water was perfectly safe if people could get to it without coming in contact with the soil.

This example clearly illustrates an important danger in *ex post facto* research: An apparent cause (in this case, the water) may be merely associated with the true cause (in this case, the soil).

Of course, for many problems such as the one we just considered, researchers have no choice but to employ the *ex post facto* method when looking for causal agents. The lesson to be learned here is *not* that this type of research should be avoided. Rather, it should be carefully conducted and interpreted with caution.

Trick or Trap 16

Testosterone Causes Aggressiveness?

Testosterone (the "male hormone") has been known to scientists for about 65 years. It has been blamed and praised for many things over the years from baldness to aggressiveness. The perceived relationship between testosterone and aggressiveness is so widespread that it is even mentioned in dictionaries. For example, the on-line WWWebster Dictionary gives as a second definition for testosterone: "qualities (as brawn and aggressiveness) usually associated with males." Thus, one could say, "He's really showing his testosterone," to imply that a male is especially aggressive.

As it turns out, there is a relationship between testosterone and aggressiveness. Here's what it is: Men have testosterone and are more aggressive than women, who do not have testosterone. Of course, one is tempted to believe that testosterone is the major source or *cause* of male aggressiveness. However, the most solid method for determining cause-and-effect relationships is to conduct *experiments* in which we manipulate something (like giving people aspirin) and observe for possible effects (like a reduction in pain).

As it turns out, some recent small-scale experiments involving testosterone have been conducted. While the experiments involve too few men and have other technical flaws, the tentative conclusions are just the opposite of what was concluded based on simple observation.

In one experiment conducted at UCLA, a small group of men with unusually low testosterone levels were treated to increase their levels. Surprisingly, as the levels were increased, the men became *less* irritable and angry.

In another experiment conducted at the Seattle Veterans Affairs Medical Center, testosterone levels in a small group of healthy males were temporarily *lowered*, with the result that the men reported *higher* levels of irritability and aggression.[1]

While the results of these experiments are highly tentative and need to be confirmed by larger-scale experiments, they do illustrate an important statistical principle: Widely accepted "facts" that are based on simple observation of an association might be incorrect. Whenever possible, experiments (in which subjects are given some treatment such as testosterone injections) should be conducted to confirm possible causal connections.

---

[1] Source: Testosterone wimping out? *Newsweek*, July 3, 1995, p. 61.

Trick or Trap 17

Liquor Outlets Cause Crime?

It has been widely observed that poorer neighborhoods have more crime and also have more liquor outlets (including bars and liquor stores) than more prosperous neighborhoods. An obvious conclusion is that liquor outlets *cause* crime. Here's one conclusion from a study that examined the association between liquor outlets and crime rates in Southern California cities: "Each liquor outlet *contributed* an average of 3.4 violent crimes a year...."[1] Notice that the word *contributed* suggests causality—that liquor outlets cause crime. In addition, other researchers have speculated that more liquor outlets cause more alcohol consumption, which leads to more crime.

However, a little thought suggests that the presence of more liquor outlets in poorer neighborhoods might be the *result* of the higher alcohol consumption in poor areas and not the *cause*. For example, those interested in opening liquor stores may be drawn to poor areas with higher per capita alcohol consumption patterns. Thus, the presence of large numbers of liquor stores might only be a *sign* of the consumption and associated crime, not its cause.

While the observed association between the number of liquor outlets and crime rates is solid, whether there is a cause-and-effect connection has not been definitively determined. To establish such a connection in which we can have great confidence, an experiment would be needed in which more liquor outlets are assigned at random to some neighborhoods than to other *comparable* neighbor-

---

[1] Source: Crime rate and liquor outlets tied. *Los Angeles Times*, May 1, 1995, pp. B1 & B3.

hoods. The two groups of neighborhoods should, of course, be comparable in terms of poverty, home ownership, unemployment rates, and so on. If the neighborhoods with more liquor outlets then exhibit higher crime rates, we would have evidence that points the finger at liquor outlets. Short of this type of study, the question of causality will not be definitively answered.

While the question of cause-and-effect regarding liquor outlets and crime is still subject to debate, there are many other associations that lead to obviously questionable, and sometimes humorous, causal conclusions. Table 1 shows a few.

Table 1 *Some observed relationships and questionable causal connections*

Observed relationship:
We see more umbrellas when it rains than when it's clear.
Causal conclusion:
Umbrellas cause rain.
Observed relationship:
A higher percentage of people are dead when they leave hospitals than the percentage that are dead when they leave other public buildings.
Causal conclusion:
Hospital personnel kill people.
Observed relationship:
People talk more about how hungry they are when they are in restaurants than when they are in other business establishments.
Causal conclusion:
Restaurants cause hunger.

Trick or Trap 18

Soybeans or Animal Fat?

Too much LDL or "bad" cholesterol is believed to be a major risk factor in coronary heart disease. Much research has been conducted on how to lower this type of cholesterol with special attention to the effects of cholesterol-lowering drugs and the effects of diet.

In particular, soybean protein, which comes in forms such as tofu, has been of interest as a possible agent for lowering cholesterol. Recently, statisticians examined 38 previous studies on the effects of a soybean-rich diet. Taken as a whole, these studies indicated that *substituting soybean products for animal fat* even for a short time cuts cholesterol levels by about nine percent.[1] Although drugs typically are somewhat more effective than this, many people would prefer a "natural" cure.

---

[1] Source: Soy protein diet cuts cholesterol, study finds. *Los Angeles Times*, August 3, 1995, p. A8.

Based on this review of previous studies, one expert stated that increasing consumption of soy equals decreased chances of coronary heart disease. This particular statement is potentially misleading because of *confounding* in the studies. *Confounding* is a scientific term that refers to statistical studies in which there are two or more explanations for a given outcome. In the studies that were reviewed, there was one outcome: reduced cholesterol. However, there are three possible explanations for the outcome:

(1) increased intake of soy caused it.

(2) decreased intake of animal fat caused it.

(3) increased intake of soy *in conjunction with* decreased intake of animal fat caused it.

Why is this important? Because if there are three possible explanations, then there are three possible courses of action people might take to reduce their cholesterol. For example, if explanation number 2 (decreased intake of animal fat) is true, you might not need soy at all—just a decrease in animal fat. On the other hand, if explanation number 3 is correct, eating soy *without* decreasing animal fat may *not* help.

The general principle here is that if two or more treatments are given at the same time to the same subjects in an experiment, there will be a confounding that makes it impossible to definitively identify the effects of each treatment separately. This problem could have been avoided in the experiments if four groups had been established with:

(1) Group 1: Maintains a normal diet but supplementing it with soy.

(2) Group 2: Maintains a normal diet by reducing animal fat.

(3) Group 3: Supplements diet with soy and reduces animal fat.

(4) Group 4: No change in diet (control group).

Trick or Trap 19

Does Designated Driving Work?

In recent years, designated driver programs have been heavily promoted. As you know, the idea is for one person in a group to be designated as the driver who will abstain from drinking alcohol. These programs have been endorsed by numerous organizations and high-level officials such as the President of the United States. Some critics, however, suggest that the programs actually encourage drinking (among those not designated as a driver) and that increased alcohol consumption has many negative social, personal, and health consequences.

At first glance, statistics support the contention that the programs are effective. For example, in 1998, alcohol was involved in 15,936 traffic fatalities (38.4% of the total), which is the lowest level since the government began tracking this in

1975.[1] As points of comparison, there were about 28,000 such fatalities in 1980 and 17,461 in 1993.[2]

Unfortunately, the conclusion that designated driver programs are responsible for the decline is *confounded* by other variables that may have contributed to the reduction. Let's consider a few of the potentially important ones.

First, during the period that the designated driver programs were being promoted, 17 states enacted laws that restrict driving by teenagers at night when teenagers are most likely to drink and drive. For example, the state of New York generally prohibits driving by those under 18 years of age between 9 P.M. and 5 A.M. In addition, most states have enacted much lower permitted blood alcohol levels for teenage drivers, with some states permitting none (that is, anything above 0.0 makes a teenager guilty of driving under the influence).

Another confounding variable is increased use of seat belts. For example, seat-belt use rose from 62.2% in 1997 to 65.1% in 1998 (when measured in both years around the Memorial Day holiday). Whether people are drinking-and-driving or not, increased seat-belt use reduces fatalities,[3] which could help to account for the decline in alcohol-related traffic fatalities during the period in which designated driver programs were being promoted.

Third, alcohol consumption in general has been declining during the period in question. While the reasons for this are not clear, reduced consumption of alcohol in general is a good candidate for helping to explain a decrease in alcohol-related traffic fatalities.

By now, it should be obvious that attempting to determine the effectiveness of designated driver programs in reducing alcohol-related traffic fatalities is exceedingly difficult because whatever effect these programs have are *co-mingled* (or *confounded*) with the effects of other factors that may also have a large impact on the outcome.

Clearly, the way to avoid confounding is to try one treatment at a time (such as promoting designated driving in selected cities), ideally with a control group (such as comparable cities) that do not receive the treatment. Unfortunately, this is not possible when evaluating programs that are promoted at the national level.

---

[1] Source: National Highway Traffic Safety Administration.

[2] Source: Designated driving programs may neglect costs of alcohol. *Los Angeles Times*, June 20, 1995, p. A5.

[3] This claim is based on the estimates that while a majority wears seat belts, about 62% of those killed in automobile accidents are from the minority that are *not* wearing them. Source: www.insure.com.

Trick or Trap 20

Predicting a Presidential Election?

During presidential elections, the press often runs short reports on factors that might predict the outcome of an election—based on the outcomes of previous elections. Let's consider two examples from the presidential cycle in which Bill Clinton was being challenged by Bob Dole.

First, *Time* magazine reported that "The candidate who appeared on screen to the left of his major opponent in the first debate has typically won the election. The one exception: Ronald Reagan."[1] This was reported shortly before the 1996 election. Up to that point, there had been only nine presidential elections with televised debates, so the winner had been on the left seven times and on the right twice. In 1996, Bob Dole was on the left during the first debate and lost, so the score became seven to three. Even at seven to three, the odds still favor the candidate on the left, but would you stake the family fortune by betting on the candidate on the left in the next election without even knowing who the candidates will be? If you answered no, you probably recognized a fundamental problem with these statistics: *the sample is too small.* With very small samples, it's easy for coincidental relationships to emerge.

In the second example, *Newsweek* pointed out that every time the New York Yankees won the World Series during an election year, the Republican candidate has won the White House.[2] However, up to the point that the election was held, the

---

[1] Source: Location, location, location. *Time*, October 21, 1996 (p. 26).
[2] Source: One last hope for Bob Dole. *Newsweek*, October 28, 1996 (p. 6).

Yanks had played in the World Series only five presidential election years. Both they and the Republicans won in 1952 and 1956, and both lost in 1960, 1964, and 1976. Once again, the sample is obviously too small to draw reliable conclusions. Also notice that there is no reason in theory to expect the outcome of the World Series to be related to the outcome of a presidential election. This is important because a finding based on a very small sample that has no basis in logic or theory is especially suspicious.

The reporters undoubtedly knew that these were unreliable predictors of the presidential elections and presented the reports as interesting asides. Yet, many people find it all too easy to fall into the trap of generalizing from a very small sample to reach a broader conclusion. For example, suppose you visited a distant city on vacation and got robbed on the street. Would you be tempted to generalize from this sample of just one visit that the city is especially dangerous? Sound statistical reasoning would require much more comprehensive statistics before allowing such a conclusion.

Trick or Trap 21

Franklin Roosevelt a Loser?

Students of American history know that Franklin Roosevelt was one of the most popular presidents—winning election to the presidency four times in a row. Yet, there was a point in time when many thoughtful people believed that the statistical evidence was running against him.

In a nutshell, here's what happened. The *Literary Digest* mailed out 10,000,000 questionnaires concerning the 1936 presidential election. About 2,400,000 people responded, and they indicated a clear preference for Alfred Landon, the Republican who was running against Roosevelt in his reelection bid.

Despite the incredible size of the sample contacted and the large number of respondents, the poll was dead wrong. Roosevelt won handily. Why was the poll so inaccurate? Part of the answer lies in how the original 10,000,000 people were selected. The *Literary Digest* obtained its mailing list primarily from telephone listings and automobile registration lists. Note that in 1936, the country was in the midst of the Great Depression, so telephones and automobiles were not as widespread as they are today. In addition, those who had them tended to be wealthier, and the wealthy tended to be Republican. So the poll was *biased* since it tended to favor Republicans over Democrats.

The other part of the answer lies in the self-selection of respondents. Only about 24% (2,400,000) of the people responded, that is, they self-selected to respond while others did not. Considerable research on public opinion polling since that time strongly suggests that in response to mailed polls, people from higher socioeconomic status groups are more likely to respond. Thus, the self-selection of respondents (another source of *bias*) tended to favor the Republicans.

At the same time, other polls, including one conducted by George Gallup using about 56,000 respondents, correctly predicted that Roosevelt would win. These other polls were correct in calling the election because they avoided serious sources of bias such as those in the *Literary Digest* poll. As you may know, pollsters today conduct national surveys and get rather accurate results using only about 1,500 respondents. This is possible by concentrating on getting a good cross section of the voting population rather than using a large sample. So the lesson is clear: Having a sample that is free of bias is much more important than having a large sample. More concretely, asking millions of the wrong people gives you a wrong answer millions of times over.

While professional polling organizations today go to great lengths to avoid the trap we are considering, if you review the survey research reported in academic journals, it will be easy to find numerous reports on mail surveys to which there are low (self-selected) rates of return. Most of this research is conducted by professors who have limited resources for conducting follow-ups and contacting people in person. In fact, many of them argue that a return rate of 60% or more is "acceptable." Despite this claim, considerable caution should be used in interpreting such reports, keeping in mind that professional polling organizations aim for response rates of 90% or more.[1]

---

[1] Today, because telephones are in widespread use even among the poor, conducting polls by calling people on the telephone usually results in reasonably accurate results, and usually yields a much higher response rate than mailed questionnaires. Note that pollsters prefer to use "random-digit dialing," that is, dialing numbers selected at random (like drawing names out of a hat) so that even those with unlisted telephone numbers are included in the surveys.

Trick or Trap 22

Bias All Around Us?

   If you read Trick or Trap 21, you already appreciate the seriousness with which a bias should be treated when considering the results of surveys. However, you may not realize how pervasive bias in sampling is. Here we'll consider a few examples of different types of bias.

- You've probably all seen polls in magazines, on TV, and on the Internet. All are clearly subject to self-selection, with those most interested in a topic most likely to respond. In addition, only those who self-select to view or read the medium in which the polls appear have a chance to respond. Here's an example of a poll with results that run counter to the best statistical information available on the topic: A major newspaper requested responses on housework and how it is divided between husbands and wives. It reported that "More than half of the 72 replies were glowing tributes to husbands who mop floors, scrub toilets...and more."[1] It's probably best to think of such polls as "That's Entertainment." It's great if reading them brings you enjoyment, but keep in mind that they are likely to be highly biased and not a basis for estimating what is going on in the general population.

- There's a saying that "much of what we know about psychology is based on the behavior of college sophomores." This is because students who take introductory psychology are often required to participate in psychological studies. Various types of studies are announced, and students self-select a study in which to participate. Often, an entire line of investigation is based solely on such students. For example, a team of researchers recently conducted a study on lying in various types of relationships. In their introduction, they pointed out that their "community sample" was the *first* "in the literature on lying in everyday life that is not a group consisting solely of college students."[2] Of course, there will be times when psychologists are especially interested in the problems of college students and appropriately study only them. However, when psychologists study broader issues with reference to the general population, their data is contaminated by a bias in favor of college students.

- Finally, there's the possibility of deliberate bias—where someone deliberately selects respondents who are most likely to support a certain outcome. A recent example was reported by researchers at the University of Minnesota who found that some schools try to keep students with learning disabilities from participating in statewide testing.[3] In some cases, these students are sent on field trips or are told to stay home on the testing day. To the extent this is true, the sample is biased against lower achievers, which results in higher overall scores. Higher scores, of course, make the schools look better.

---

[1] Source: *The Houston Chronicle*, September 23, 1990, p. G1. (Posted on the Internet by Jurg Gerber.)
[2] Source: DePaulo, B. M. & Kashy, D. A. (1998). Everyday lies in close and casual relationships. *Journal of Personality and Social Psychology, 74,* 63–79.
[3] Source: Why Johnny stayed home. *Newsweek*, October 6, 1997, p. 60.

Trick or Trap 23

Whom Do You Trust?

The research in the social and behavioral sciences abounds with self-reports. Respondents are asked to "tell on themselves" about all kinds of things from stealing and lying to helping elderly ladies cross the street.

Self-reports are widely used because they are efficient and inexpensive. Simply write some questions, duplicate and distribute them in a college classroom, for example, and *presto*, data for statistical analysis have been generated.

Of course, the results of the statistical analysis are only as solid as the truthfulness of the self-reports. To increase the odds that respondents will be truthful, researchers often assure their respondents that their responses will be confidential and/or anonymous. Even under these circumstances, however, respondents may not be truthful for a variety of reasons. For example, they may not believe the assurances of confidentiality/anonymity, they may be in denial, they may not want to tell the truth under any circumstances, or they may have simply forgotten what they have done. Despite these possibilities, researchers often take the respondents at their word. However, some researchers recognize that this can be dangerous. Here are two examples:

• Some careful researchers try to confirm the validity of the self-reports they collected. In one interesting study, researchers were evaluating a driving-under-the-influence component of the instructional programs at driving schools.[1] An essential element was to determine whether the students were driving under the influence after being exposed to the component. First, they asked the students to self-report on this behavior. Then, for a sample of 62 of the students who claimed they had *not* driven while intoxicated, the researchers contacted the students' friends and relatives. According to these people, seven (11%) of the 62 had, indeed, driven while intoxicated. Now whom do you trust? If you think the reports of the friends and relatives are more likely to be accurate than the reports of the students, then a sizable minority of the students gave false self-reports.

- In their review of the extensive literature on the relationship between teacher stress and health, researchers pointed out most of the data on their health is based only on self-reports, which the reviewers call the "single-method trap." This refers to using only a single method to measure a variable.[2] They point out that some researchers have avoided this by using a multimethod approach (using more than just self-reports as in our previous example). For example, in addition to self-reports, symptoms of illness were measured by one research team using physiological measures such as cholesterol levels and blood pressure. Other researchers have supplemented self-reports by examining the number of sick days taken (recognizing, of course, that some teachers may not actually be sick when they take sick days).

There are two lessons here. First, self-reports on sensitive issues should be taken with at least a grain of salt. Second, studies that supplement self-reports with other measures generally are stronger.

---

[1] Source: Kayser, R. E., Schippers, G. M., & Van Der Staak, C. P. F. (1995). Evaluation of a Dutch educational "driving while intoxicated" (DWI) prevention program for driving schools. *Journal of Drug Education, 25*, 379–393.
[2] Source: Guglielmi, R. S. & Tatrow, K. (1998). Occupational stress, burnout, and health in teachers: A methodological and theoretical analysis. *Review of Educational Research, 68*, 61–99.

Trick or Trap 24

Valid Predictors of Achievement?

Educators routinely use tests to predict future achievement. For example, the College Board's Scholastic Aptitude Test is designed to predict achievement in college. Other tests are designed to predict success in specific skill areas such as first-grade reading and high-school algebra.

The validity of any statistical analysis based on such tests depends on the validity of the tests themselves. So how valid are such tests? In general, they are only modestly valid. Let's look at a specific example to see what this means. Suppose we gave an algebra prognosis test (a test that measures skills that will be needed in algebra) to 106 students in a small high school. Subsequently, they all took Algebra I and earned grades from A to F. Table 1 shows a distribution that one might obtain.

Table 1   Percentage of students who earned each grade in each score level

Algebra Prognosis Score	Grade Earned in the Course				
	F	D	C	B	A
40–49	0%	0%	33%	33%	33%
30–39	0%	8%	46%	15%	31%
20–29	5%	12%	39%	37%	7%
10–19	12%	35%	46%	7%	0%
0–9	33%	33%	33%	0%	0%

Inspection of Table 1 shows that the test has some measure of validity. Over-all, there is a general *tendency* for those with higher scores to earn higher grades in algebra (that is, it has some predictive validity), but notice that it is very far from being perfectly valid. Here are some cases that illustrate the point:

- A third (33%) of those in the highest scoring group earned a grade of "C" while a third of those in the lowest scoring group also earned a grade of "C."

- A larger percentage (37%) in the 20–29 score range earned a grade of "B" than the percentage in the 40–49 score range.

While the statistical data we are considering here is not for any one particular test, it is fairly typical for a standardized test designed to predict achievement. Why are such tests so far from perfect? While there are a variety of reasons, here are some of the major ones:

- All tests have some degree of unreliability due to chance factors such as guessing and students not feeling well on the day the test was administered.

- All such tests measure only a sample of the underlying skills (such as basic math skills underlying success in algebra). Sampling introduces error.

- Achievement in an academic area requires more than just cognitive skills. For example, doing homework, coming to class, and being conscientious when taking classroom tests used for grading also affect the grades students earn.

The lesson to be learned here is that standardized tests are almost always far from perfect in their validity. Thus, results should be interpreted very cautiously and supplemented with other sources of information such as teachers' ratings and evaluations of students' work such as term papers.

Trick or Trap 25

Achieving at Grade Level?

GRADE LEVEL

If newspaper reports regarding grade-level achievement are to be believed, America's schools are doing a dismal job. For example, in large cities it is not uncommon to read that 60%–70% of students are achieving below grade level in important areas such as reading and math. Even in the affluent suburbs, it's common to find that 30%–40% are below grade level.

Before we can assess the seriousness of these apparent deficiencies, we need to consider how "grade level" is defined statistically. Let's say you are building a standardized test in reading for use nationally at the third-grade level. First, you would need to determine what is being taught at that level. Since we do not have a national curriculum, you would need to examine a sample of the third-grade in-structional objectives in math developed by various school districts throughout the nation and create a synthesis of them on which to base your test. Already, you can see the potential for error—students in a school district that has objectives that de-viate significantly from your synthesis may be penalized by your test.

Then, you need to write and try out test items and assemble them into a test. For slower students, you will want to start the test with some easy items (even if the test content is below the third-grade level) and end the test with some difficult items to challenge more advanced students (even if the test content is above the third-grade level). Then, you will need to select a small number of items of medium difficulty (say, 25 items) since third-grade students won't be able to sit still and concentrate on a much larger number of items. Using only a small sample of possible third-grade math items introduces yet another potential source of error. (Also notice that not all the items are even at the third-grade level.)

Next, you need to establish statistically the grade-equivalent (grade-level) norms by trying out your test with a national sample of students who are just beginning the third grade as well as a sample who have just finished the third grade (called a "norm group"). To keep it simple, let's just consider the sample at the end of third grade (that is, grade 3.9, which means the ninth month of the third grade). Suppose that these students get an average number-right of 17. Then, all students with 17 right will be assigned a grade-equivalent score of 3.9. Since this is based on an average, about 50% of the students will be assigned grade-equivalents above 3.9, and the other half will be assigned grade-equivalents below grade level. (This result will be used in assigning grade equivalents to other students with whom the test is subsequently used.) So you can see that in a representative national sample of students in grade 3.9, *half* are below grade level and *half* are above grade level—*by definition*. That is, when the test is built, for statistical purposes, half the students are automatically below grade level.

What does this mean when your test is subsequently used around the country with students in grade 3.9? First, a district that has 50% of its students scoring below 3.9 is *average* in comparison with your national sample. (In other words, you assigned grade-equivalents of less than 3.9 to 50% of the representative national sample when you built your test. A district that has this same result is representative of the national average on your test.) Second, a district that has 60% with grade-equivalents below 3.9 needs to pull up only 10% of its students above 3.9 to become average, which is not nearly as dismal as it might initially seem.

If you're finding it difficult to follow this line of reasoning, just remember this: Nationally, half the students must be below grade level because of the way the grade-equivalent scores are statistically derived. Even if all third-grade students in the nation greatly improved their math skills, new editions of the test would be published and, because of the standardization procedure, half would again be assigned to being "below grade level" by the test makers at the time the new editions are produced.

Trick or Trap 26

Are You an Individual?

Arguably, the most dangerous and blatant trick or trap in statistics is to cite the results of just one study on a topic without regard to the findings of the larger body of research on that topic.

As an example, let's consider the body of research on aggression and *deindividuation*. Deindividuation occurs when people become at least partially anonymous by acting as part of a larger group or by having their individual identities hidden by masks or hoods. In a review of the body of research on this topic, the following example was cited:[1]

In an early laboratory study on deindividuation (Zimbardo, 1969), female participants were randomly assigned to one of two groups. In the deindividuated group, participants wore large lab coats, wore hoods over their heads, and were not referred to by name. In the individuated group, participants did not wear lab coats, wore large name tags, and were referred to by name.

Participants in both groups were asked to give electric shocks to another person. The researcher found that those in the deindividuated group gave longer shocks than those in the other group.[2]

---

[1] Source: Anderson, C. A. & Bushman, B. J. (1997). External validity of "trivial" experiments: The case of laboratory aggression. *Review of General Psychology*, *1*, 19–41.

[2] In this type of study, shocks are not actually given; however, participants *think* they are giving shocks.

After citing the above example, the reviewers point out that "a number of subsequent laboratory studies have shown that aggression is increased when participants are placed in a deindividuated state." They cite 14 studies conducted by a number of different investigators and published between 1975 and 1994 as the basis for this statement. However, they note that two studies (published in 1978 and 1979) failed to confirm this finding.

What should we make of the discrepancy between the 14 studies showing a difference and the two that do not? As a general rule, we should rely on the larger group of studies for guidance. The main exception is if someone could show that the 14 studies were all subject to serious traps or tricks, while the two in the minority were more statistically sound. (We'll take up this consideration in Trick or Trap 27.)

The potential *trap* here is that someone may be aware of only one study, and cite its results by saying, "Such and such a study (one particular study) *proves* blah blah blah blah blah." Beware when an instructor, supervisor, or someone else makes such a statement. Statistical research provides *degrees of evidence*, not *proof*. In addition, on most important topics, there are a number of studies that might be (and should be) cited. The potential *trick* is when someone is fully aware of the larger body of research but cites only a particular study in the minority (such as one of the two studies mentioned above) in order to deliberately mislead his or her listeners. Your best defense against these tricks and traps is to ask about the trends in the larger body of statistical research on the topic of interest. In other words, *look at the big picture* before drawing conclusions.

Trick or Trap 27

Families and Drug Treatment?

In Trick or Trap 26, you learned the value of looking at the big picture when considering a topic that has been investigated statistically. The "big picture" results from considering what the majority of studies on a given topic indicate.

By now, however, you also know that all statistical studies are subject to a wide variety of pitfalls, so when looking at the big picture, it pays to consider the *quality* of the individual studies that are being considered as a group.

Let's consider an example of how this was recently done by some professors who reviewed the research on using family therapy with drug abusers.[1] They conducted a search of the statistical literature to locate studies in which the primary concern was abuse of or addiction to illicit drugs (not alcohol). To qualify, a study needed to include family therapy (including couples-therapy) and at least one other type of therapy for comparison purposes.

---

[1] Source: Stanton, M. D. & Shadish, W. R. (1997). Outcome, attrition, and family-couples treatment for drug abuse: A meta-analysis and review of the controlled, comparative studies. *Psychological Bulletin*, *122*, 170–191.

To control for *quality*, they considered only studies in which participants were assigned *at random* to the different types of therapy. *At random* is equivalent to drawing names out of a hat to determine which type of therapy each participant received. Why is this important? Because if participants self-select into one kind of therapy or another, the groups might be substantially different from each other in terms of drug use, amenability to therapy, and other important ways. Put another way, random assignment prevents a bias in the assignment of participants to groups. The reviewers stated it this way: Requiring random assignment for a study to be included was done "to minimize ambiguity and maximize the confidence that could be placed in any conclusions that might emerge...." In all, 15 "quality" studies were identified. Reviewing these 15 "quality studies" permitted the professors to summarize their review with some confidence as follows:

> This review synthesizes drug abuse outcome studies that included a family-couples therapy treatment condition. The...evidence across 1,571 cases involving an estimated 3,500 patients and family members favors family therapy over (a) individual counseling or therapy, (b) peer group therapy, and (c) family psychoeducation. Family therapy is as effective for adults as for adolescents.

The lesson here is that despite all the possible statistical tricks and traps, knowledge can be advanced with statistical research if we keep our eye on the big picture—with special attention to studies that meet standards for high quality.

Notes:

Notes:

Notes: